Mother Poems and
A Crack in Time

JAYA KULA PRESS BOOKS BY
SHAMBHAVI SARASVATI

Pilgrims to Openness: Direct Realization Tantra in Everyday Life, 2009

The Play of Awakening: Adventures on the Path of Direct Realization Tantra, 2012

Returning: Exhortations, Advice and Encouragement from the Heart of Direct Realization Practice, 2015

No Retreat: Poems on the Way to Waking Up, 2016

Nine Poisons, Nine Medicines, Nine Fruits, 2017

The Reality Sutras: Seeking the Heart of Trika Shaivism, 2018

Mother Poems and A Crack in Time, 2025

Mother Poems and
A Crack in Time

Shambhavi Sarasvati

JAYA KULA PRESS

Jaya Kula Press
3439 NE Sandy Blvd. #859
Portland, Oregon 97232
jayakula.org

© 2025 by Shambhavi Sarasvati

All rights reserved. No part of this book may be reproduced in any form, or by any means, without permission in writing from the publisher.

Cover design: Sandra Friesen and Shambhavi Sarasvati

Interior design and layout: Sandra Friesen
www.sandrafriesen.com

Library of Congress Control Number:
2025903970

Sarasvati, Shambhavi
Mother Poems and A Crack in Time

978-1-7322183-4-5 (PBK)
979-8-3507-4488-0 (EBK)

Printed in the United States of America on acid-free paper.

For the people of Gaza and all who seek liberation

Contents

Introduction	xi

MOTHER POEMS

Mixed Bag	1
Speak	2
Will It Come to Me?	3
Advice to Myself	6
Yugas	7
Be Loyal to Wisdom	9
Every Day	10
Frozen Lake	12
I Am for Ma	14
Not a God	16
Seeds of Dharma in the Western-Seeming Zones	18
Seeds of Worship	20
A Traveler's Unreasonable True Dream	22
Avalanche Prayer	24
Spiritual Biz Flu	25
Don't Budge	26
Sixty-Five Prayer	27
What I Miss	28
Cave Retreat	31
Stop Deciding	32
This Longing to Know You	33

Not This Not That	34
I Follow the Ruler of My Heart	35
Jump	36
Coming in Like This	38
Because I Am This	39
The Sweet Taste	41
Since You Cannot Hear	43
Words Fail	45
Multiverse	46
Only Her	47
End of a Moon	48
Becoming Moon	49
All the Others	50
Only Those	51
Temporary	52
Alone with You	53
Sitters	54
God the Enjoyer	55
Because No One Taught Me Your Names	56
Navigation by Scent	59
Let Me Be the Incense	61

A CRACK IN TIME

Gaza Mo(u)rning	64
I Have a Catalog in My Heart	65
Speechless Poem for Speechless Time	67
Things Worshippers Must See and Hear	68
Salt Water	70
Jewels of God	72
Humanity in Tents	74
When We Come to Rafah	75

You Are Not Coming	77
Spring in Portland	79
Petrichor Heartbreak	80
The Tortilla Survival Protocol	81
What They Carry	83
Fresh Magic	85
Aging Revolutionary	86
Rations	87
303 Days	89
336 Days	90
Motaz Wrote	91
I Realize This is Not a Poem	92
Don't Let Me Look	93
Day 277 Exquisite Corpse	95
Tenderness in the Rubble	96
Another Sweet Boy is Dead	97
Suzy and the Genociders	98
Those Who Cannot Tolerate Beauty	100
Drowning and Jasmine	102
Blast Zone	103
We Run to Us	104
Acknowledgments	107
About Shambhavi	108

Introduction

When I first encountered the poetry of the great 19th-century Kali devotee, Ramprasad Sen, I was shocked to find him railing at his beloved form of the divine. Ramprasad often complains of being condemned by the Goddess to both literal and spiritual poverty. The poetic sayings of the 14th-century Kashmiri yogini, Lal Ded, movingly reveal her pain at being stung by the fierce words of her teacher and of times when she feels spiritually inadequate. Occasionally, Lal Ded openly mocks other practitioners who she believes are misguided in their views.

I began writing *Mother Poems* during a turbulent time in my spiritual life. Much of the turmoil resulted from the inner churning that inevitably brings more growth. But the global pandemic and other external circumstances intensified feelings of dissatisfaction and alienation. Composers of spiritual poetry from India, such as Ramprasad and Lal Ded, give us permission to express anger, sadness, and frustration alongside more conventional devotional feelings. They show us that our highly personal relationships with God and Guru do not demand that we exile any variety of human expression. The Mother or Ma who I sometimes urgently call upon in these poems is my Guru. She is also the divine Mother. And she is simultaneously the all-pervasive wisdom.

On October 7, 2023, another turbulence erupted. My poetry and other writings took a sharp turn toward exploring my responses to the first live-streamed genocide in human history.

A Crack in Time is an outpouring of tenderness and wonder, of horror and grief. It lays bare the pain of coming to greater clarity. It enumerates crimes and speaks innumerable pleas for the people of Palestine and the world. It documents the advent of a period of intense destruction that opens a space for transformation: a crack in time.

In keeping with the view of my traditions, most of my teaching and writing seeks to convey the reality that there is no divide between the spiritual and the mundane. Everything is imbued with the supreme intelligence. Any aspect of manifest life can deliver us to greater wisdom.

These two groups of poems contain much of what could be called prayer. While always devotional, they attempt to bring disruption, doubt, cruelty, and chaos onto our paths of awakening. I gathered them together in one book as a modest demonstration that all aspects of life are connected, and so are we.

with infinite love,
Shambhavi
Portland, Oregon

Mother Poems

Mixed Bag

Today I felt
feverish and exhausted
horny and exalted
devoted and resistant
maligned and totally supported.
For no reason, I nearly vomited
and the subtle channels
were unusually receptive.
This is all true
without a speck of
poetry or
elaboration.

Speak

Ma, wherever you take me
is where I want to go
whether to fame or ignominy
whether beaten or praised
whether I have a fat bank account
or am living day to day.

It's all fine
but please speak up
in words tuned to these ears
so this know-nothing
can hear, understand and
follow behind.

Will It Come to Me?

Will it come to me?
A friendly way to live in samsara?
So far no dice.

I wander around in dreams
visiting cities, towns
seasides and markets
in unknown times.

I talk to strangers and
lend a helping hand.
Then I'm gone
or sleep is.

Dreamtime is wandering free
but daylight brings
obstinate minds
walled houses and
other simulacra of
the longing for
eternal life.

I chide myself:
Stop complaining!
Everything's perfect!
All phenomena are equal!
Samsara and nirvana the same!

Awake and dreaming both magical displays!
Even having seen this for myself
I still want out.

Last night, day
invaded the dark.
In my dream
a student piled
shopping, schoolwork and
shoes on the floor around the
worship place.

While cleaning up
I yelled:
An altar is no place for this mess!
All over the house
students had replaced my
offerings with the resilient detritus
of their lives.

A team of rough men posing as
inspectors barged in.
They rifled through everything.
When asked for identification,
they puffed out their chests and glared.
I woke with a strangled cry.

My teachers say it's good
when everyday appearings
become intolerable

and one loses the taste
for the mundane
even for waking up.

I pray to receive the teaching about
whatever comes
after this.

Advice to Myself

Answer everyone
from the cave of the heart.

Don't waste energy arguing with
those who cling to skepticism
rectitude
and books.

Stop exhausting yourself pulling
at what holds them to the forced way.
Their chains are also God.

Remain small and receptive
like a homeless person
lingering at the door.
You never know when the inmates
might call out
and ask to share in
the Meal.

Yugas

The door to this prison is open
but few ever step out.
They talk about the
furniture obsessively.
They breathe dense air
and their own nervous
perfumes.

In certain waking dreams
people come gunning
with their urgency and laws.
They aim their criticisms and
demands at anyone who
evades their worldview.

I hide out
gently breathing, unseen.
If someone notices
I share whatever medicines
I've received.
Otherwise, I don't stop them
from leaving
and I get on with
my real life.

I used to fight for everyone
including myself.

That was easier.
Now I'm an escape artist
who understands she has
nowhere to go.
If I want to live in another world
it will have to be right here
with everything
exactly
as it is.

Be Loyal to Wisdom

To a student who asked me about loyalty:
Be loyal to wisdom.
Freedom is not
your own way.
Freedom is the supreme
improvisational following.

Stop striving to find your dharma.
Nothing belongs to you.
Relax and let wisdom sweep away
all compulsions and constructions.

Despite these words, you'll likely go on
loyal to your plans and names
loyal to logic and conceptions.
You'll go on making stronger versions of yourself
mistaking that for realization.

I don't know how more plainly
I can say.
Live like a dragon in the sky!
Live like a wild mare upon the ground!
Live like a human traveler walking maps
written in the water
and the sky.

Every Day

Every day we choose some clothes.
But if we are too attached to appearances
then in all this magical display
there's nothing to enjoy.

If we have enough
yet worry about getting more
then despite the miracle of being alive
happiness eludes us.

If times seem hard
and we rail against them
fear distorts clear seeing and
we cannot skillfully cross
the river of circumstance.

Living or dying
if we care too much about
the times behind us
we cannot gain the fruits of
this supreme passage.

Life renews constantly
like waves riding to shore.
But if we only want to grow and maintain
while rejecting subsidence
our suffering will drown us.

Our Mother is
the living light
of infinite circumstance.
We rest in Her
awake, dreaming, living or
dying.

If you have recognized this
try to remember
in every moment every day.
To do this is our sole aim
no matter what is happening.

Frozen Lake

We can't travel anywhere
while hiding.
We can't arrive home
with carefully managed steps.
If we shutter our eyes
we see patterns only of
our own making.

The great secret of the Self
is how generously life appears.
The great appearing of the Self
makes bodies hum.
The great pleasure of the Self is
I AM.

Reality's lake births
ungovernable forms and
styles of moving.
Desperate for the
cover of winter
some of us try to freeze
that wild generation.

But failure and time arrive
without permission.
The sun gifts early light
to the frozen surface of the lake.

Ice cracks and moves.
From winter's cold
spring does come.

God's mercy is this:
Not even the most determined among us
can command Her
unbound joy.

I Am for Ma

I saw in my body
a thousand cities
crowded with beings caught
in the wheel of time.
So I replaced them
with the sound of Ma
and the letters of Ma and
Her crystalline mind.

I saw my energy and heart
traveling here and there
trying too hard to tear down
the fragile homes
of people's anger, fear, and doubt.
So I took refuge in
namo namah shivaya
and om.

I saw how I sometimes abandoned my seat
just to make a way in the world
with false missions
no matter how well-meant
fueled by forgetting that
I am Hers alone.

Today I am a leaf in the branches of her tree.
As She is also the wind
I pray only She can move me.

Today I am sitting
at the base of her throne
Her foot on my crown
and I pray only she can still me.

Now whatever I do or don't do
in this crowded place, I ask
to always remember
I am for Ma.

Not a God

Not being a God
is a problem
only for those
who feel small.

Enjoying yourself
as you are
reflects the divine state.

The face of immodesty
sneers when
others fall short
of some invented ideal.

Convinced you are failing
you sting
with the poison
of outrageous demands.

Do you want to become a God or
bring the Gods down?
Both.

You carry on with your
fantasy, skepticism
and contempt.

This is the harm
peculiar to our age.

I sit on the ground with the learners—
the apprentices
not the Masters.
We fall readily
on knees
of curiosity, tenderness
and prayer.

Call us by any name.
Doubt our sincerity.
Cut us down to measurable size.
Beat us with the sticks of your
outrage and grief.

Our lineages cross
time and place.
We give to anyone
kind enough
to let us in
anyone at all
until the cycles turn
until more beings kneel
beside us to receive
this infinite
outpouring
of natural gifts.

Seeds of Dharma in the Western-Seeming Zones

When we say "classical"
that is violent and
self-authorizing.

When we say "origin"
we erase forgotten
people's words.

When we say "traditional"
we should mention brokenness
and not knowing.

When we say "authentic"
we are not entirely so.

Seeds of wisdom blow around
native to wherever beings
make teachers
of earth, water, fire, wind, and sky.

These seeds are never born
and they never fully bloom
in the pages of books
no matter how old or wise.

Until we meet the
barefoot walkers
lighting fires and
offering water to the land
drawing yantras from their hearts
and chanting mantras heard
directly from the sky

until we see the Buddha fields
luminous with
the primordial light
only mimicked by our sun,
the real history
and destination of seeds
remains unknown.

Let's just walk
with the barefoot ones
heads down
in supplication, study
offerings and prayer.

Let our honesty
be so strong
it calls the seeds to grow
emerging naturally from the
one pervasive ground.

Seeds of Worship

All forms of worship
are worshipped by that one
who is also the devotee
of every worshipper.

From the perspective of prayers
borders are farce
and origins cannot be told
with ordinary words.

Prayers are seeds
that travel around.
They don't mind
who speaks them
with what accent
or from where.
They wait tenderly
and bloom their scent gladly
finding the gates of the heart
even slightly ajar.

All symbols are that one's—
all scriptures and all
stories about the nature of
beings and things.

The living expanse
emits infinite rays.
Here in this crowded
City of the Heart
every meeting
finds itself
welcomed and
at home.

A Traveler's Unreasonable True Dream

You might be happier if
you immediately turn in
your attachments
to endings and beginnings
origins and destinations.

God is a recycler.
Everything perpetually turns into everything else.
Call that one the plane of becoming or
the absolute.
No difference.
Just toss your beginnings and endings
anywhere into space.
Nothing is ever truly lost.

We are all always on the move—
travelers with
so many arrivals and departures
they amount only to
the beauty of traveling
and the tenderness of sharing
stories of traveling.

Various travelers however
have not learned these simple facts.
We call them colonizers, conquerors
and collectors.

If we all learned the art of traveling
of hosting and guesting
we could live anywhere
in a borderless land.

Our bodies do not end at our skin.
Our streets and lands have no names that remain.
The host and the guest are inseparable.
All plants are native, along with all that appears here.

I want to grow kindness
instead of timelines.
I want to live among gardeners and servants and friends
not landlords and conquerors.

C'mon!
Let's rename this place Café Earth and
just laze around
without contrivances or
convictions.
If we just relax a little more
we'll discover we belong
everywhere.

Avalanche Prayer

Let me remember
the wisdom in
every stumble that brought me here.
And let me remain
empty-dark in the fourth
from fingers to toes to bones.
And also
let the blazing alive fill me—
an avalanche of living light.

Spiritual Biz Flu

So sick of spiritual biz
spiritual clothes
spiritual bling.
Sick of spiritual bios
and exaggerated claims.
Tired of spiritual promises
with high price tags.
Sick of spiritual poses, gazes and tattoos.
Sick of spiritual selfies
on social media feeds.
Tired of everyone's a teacher
and humble equals brag.
Sick of unearned teachings
confidently mouthed.
Over certifications, revelations
secrets and ah-maz-ing.
Completely over "enlightenment experiences" that are
one-off things.
I'm sick of my own name and my spiritual supplies.
I'm also sick of websites, workshops, Instagrams, and Zoom.
I just want to float in the river of come what may
in the Mother's lap
in the natural ease
in the living unnamed
untamed and
unadvertised.

Don't Budge

Once you've entered
the cave of the heart
don't budge no matter
who or what comes knocking!

In the center of that cave
is a golden throne.
Many-colored jewels
adorn its arms and legs.
The throne is the seat of
I AM.
The jewels are that one's
glamorous creation.

From the heart's royal room
you can greet
all the beings
in all the worlds
but only if you stay
seated there.

Sixty-Five Prayer

I no longer want crazy spiritual experiences.
I ask for guidance.
I no longer exert myself
chasing accomplishments.
I pray to continue as a servant.
I'm no longer seeking
special companions.
Just permit me to give away
all that I have gathered.

My optimism is waning.
That's been painful.
Now I use all my might
crossing the bardos of refusal
to the shores of reconciliation.

After years of happiness
recognizing the real nature
my heart is broken open
and the taste of you and you and
you grieving
hijacks my tongue
day and night.

What I Miss

Lord,
In an age of faux teachers
and the professionally aloof

In a yuga of brags and blame
When career debunkers earn twice
teaching desiccated versions
of your play

In this field of
promo initiations
and realization looks—
cold and greedy simulations
of your wide-awake love

When so-called teachers use
your skillful means deceitfully
and thwart sincere desires
of the young and old

When worshippers leave
their cushions to unseat
your more ignorant forms
and even your disciples
hold their skepticism dear

Lord,
You are here in this too
but still I long
for the time of the devotees.

I miss the time of honoring you in
all that comes and goes.
I miss the everyday palaces
of mantra and song.

I miss the sandalwood smoke
filling towns
the neighborhood dakini dance and
the ringing to worship
when more had ears.

In this age of
belief and disbelief
of overstatement and brand
you've tasked me with
attachments to an ancient invisible way
with greater confidence in your word
and subtle touch
than museums of
reasonable means.

Ma, my hand rests in yours, your feet on the threshold are the refuge where I forever place my head.

I know your manifold arisings are
all equality's way
but still I stubbornly mourn
some glory days
traced in the cave of my heart
echoing through
the prison of
linear time.

Finding you everywhere and in all, Lord, tell me:
Why must I miss you just the same?

Cave Retreat

I admire you
meditating in
rocky caves
braving damp and cold
eating grain, raw flour
and roots.

But that display is
a little extravagant
don't you think?
The cave of the heart can be
found anywhere
even here
in this ordinary house
where I sip my tea.

Stop Deciding

Stop deciding, Shambhavi!
Ask the Guru in your Heart
Ask the powers that be
Ask the wisdom of sky
Ask the dirt
Ask the lake
Ask the crow
Ask the sea
Ask ask ask
and when you hear the answer,
follow!
Unmind ephemeral doubts.
They are the scions
and sirens
of linear time.
Let them be.
Their way is
not yours.

This Longing to Know You

This longing to know you
the river
never stops
whose end is unknown
and known as the source.
When did I
abandon all maps
all self-determination
all colorful plans?
That moment is lost.
Now I just drift
in your all-encompassing touch
this constant current
gentle or fierce
plays as the waters
that move me along.

Not This Not That

Ma,
how am I supposed to live
when I don't want anything I have
and I also don't want anything I don't have?
Tell me.

I Follow the Ruler of My Heart

I don't care about rules or reasons.
I just don't care!
When it seems I do
I'm just avoiding yet another
mundane interrogation.
I follow the ruler of my heart.
She rests in the center on a golden throne.
Her smile plays
an infinitely modulating dance.
When she prompts me to move, I do!
She is everything and all that occurs.
With her trickster grin, she inquires:
Will you listen? Will you follow?
Sometimes she rolls her eyes at me or
seems to look away.
But never for an instant longer than
I need her to.

Jump

The devotees jump
eager for chances
to serve their Lord.
The mundane is glamorous to them.
The field of devotion is a festival of the heart
where the Lord sports infinite costumes
of lover, offerings, and beloved.

Any old thing sets them off:
dust on the floor, an unserved meal
the call for helpful arms and legs
or whatever the Lord asks for these days.

They've learned the natural language
of Self to Self
the way of offering
receiving
listening
and holding back.

But the students choose a different way.
If their invented quotas
are already met
or someone else doesn't measure up
if they're tired or grumpy or
hungry or pissed off
if they aren't admired and praised

or they're angling for ease
they sit
laughing too loudly or
talking too fast
belligerent or eyes downcast.
They ignore the Lord
who tenderly calls out
arms laden
heavy with grace.

Coming in Like This

I have no authority
no lineage to transmit
no story about who I might be.
A lonely child in an alien place
without support
for what mattered to me
I've wondered
how did I arrive
already seeking
the Friend?
How did I arrive
so determined to slash the veil
unafraid of impermanence
and with confidence
in a magic I did not yet
see?
How did I arrive
full of true dreams
and so desperate
to find out?

Because I Am This

Because I am this
I train to see the lights
unfurling like brilliant smoke
reaching from all to all.

At night I wake in dreams
so I can help myself wake
during the bardo of the day.

Knowing I'm not apart
I listen to wisdom's voice
speaking from behind
the display of ordinary mind.

Because my body is without end
I drop self-concepts and address
the textures and flows
filling even so-called space.

And when I'm granted
the precious sight of the fifth eye
I practice seeing what's really going on
not just in linear time.

My teacher has left
her human form
so I constantly explore
new ways to follow her lead.

I don't sit around waiting
for sudden enlightenment.
That would be dull.
I don't keep to the narrow lanes.
I experiment extravagantly with
body, energy, and mind
so I can meet *this*
however it plays.

The Sweet Taste

I want to always offer
the sweet taste
the jasmine scent
the diamond View
to my teachers
to the wisdom bringers
and all who come around.

No matter what happens
I return to this clear and
unobstructed way
entering the heart again and again
exhorting the garden to meet
the senses of anyone near.
What is so-called self-realization
compared to this?

Walking along
I forget about accomplishments.
This is not even a path!
Sometimes it's an amusement park ride
or a jump off a cliff
or a crazy slow song.
Other times I just rest quietly
within what shines.

But whatever this is
I take refuge
in the cave of the heart
the fresh green
emerging from the blue
and the fountain of light
flowing sweetly
from the core.

Since You Cannot Hear

Since you cannot hear
poems come out all over.
This is the nearest I can bring you
to the conversation in Her heart—

a vast silence
a vast flow of primordial speech
a vast poignancy
alongside unstoppable mercy and joy.

This crystalline clarity
is Her address.
It pierces those who hear
and Her compassionate
pleas rain continually on
the ears of
those who don't.

She has no pride.
She uses all means.
She humbles herself
to be heard.

O Mother, so that
more may hear
please help me
speak only

the words issuing from
the gap
in the center of
all this.

Words Fail

Failing to hear
the profound communication
words fail.
The difference cannot be made up
with explanations.

Only poems come close
to minding the gap
inviting the mind to yield its
childish demands for reasons.

The messages of poems escape
from cracks in time and mind
like smoke unfurling from
the half-remembered worship of the
deep and burning.

Pause the
predictable words.
Breathe in.
Fill yourself
with Her timeless
silvery perfume.

Multiverse

A tourist in an
alien familiar world
my heart is sad.
Dreams of humanoid
insect forms.
They're kindly and
live in rooms like ours.
Dakinis drop by
now and then
unveiling realms of
magical dance.
Later
I'm washing dishes
at the sink
while multicolored water
shines down.

Only Her

I look to the sky
There is no space
only She

I look at the
factory of infinite things
She is all

I enter the
cave of the heart and
there She sits
laughing on her golden throne

End of a Moon

At the end of a Pisces moon
at the end of a long night
out of the dark
whatever is left
births to light

Becoming Moon

When we chant
to the moon
I become the moon
and I overflow with the moon's delight
in sharing this sweetness
with all of you

But a person is not the moon! You say
Bound by such concepts
you don't yet know
that you are
becoming moon, too

All the Others

Merging my mind with the meditators
urgency dissolves in the fresh and green.

Merging my mind with the murderers
self-reference dissolves
in the radiance of rays from
the heart.

Merging my mind with the skeptics
secretly yearning and
predictable as a house
I'm a guest
waiting outside
the door.

Integrating awareness with Guru
words return to their source.
And there one meets
the fountain
offering itself without restraint
in generosity to all.

Only Those

Only those who have already heard
can hear your words.
For the others
words are dead and reasonable things.
Ma, your languaging is
so fine
like the rustlings of infinite silk
dresses
sweeping by.

Temporary

How ephemeral are promises
from even students and friends.
Self, don't be so attached to what comes and goes!

All week long I asked for help
but those mighty Gods
Comfort and Convenience
proved more worthy of following
than me.

Illusory ground dissolved inside and out.
Thank you, Ma for reminding me
I am no one
and to keep my sannyasins's vow.

Alone with You

Ma, I am alone
There's no one here
but you
One by one
the petals
of expectation
have fallen at your feet
then you swept them away

Sitters

I sit with the ones who sit
the ones sitting through all times.
We are just sitters.
Nothing to gain
but knowledge of
the pointlessness and beauty of sitting.
I feel you sitting with me, friends
or there is just this one sitting
in the glory
all along.

God the Enjoyer

God is an enjoyer and
our senses are the agents
of God's appreciation.
Slow down.
Revel in the
textures, sights, smells, sounds and
tastes of God's world.
Don't speed like a train
through God's kingdom
unless you are ready to host
the swaying movement
the vibration of wheels on track
the smell of train air
layered with
engine, folk, and food.
Immerse in the grain
of landscapes
as your senses
carry God
traveling on through.

Because No One Taught Me Your Names

Because no one taught me your names
I am free
to perceive them.

In a book
your names are the five wisdoms.
Other books say
one or thirty-six.

And how many times
have I chanted the hundred and eight
or one thousand
names of your embodied forms?

Those are great
but wondrous are
the names that shine
from the dark
from the blue
from the heart
and the moonlight sun.

Written in the colors of gems
singing out
from the subtle fullness of all
they speak themselves
into my eyes, into

my skin, into the
soles of my feet
and the cave
and the crown.

Within and without
cannot withstand this
onslaught of
visible sound.

And this is how
I came to know
these wisdoms intimately.

I call them play
and kindness and clear.
I call them curious
prankster
and joy.

I call them
reverence and
the unbound.

I call them
generosity and
brilliance without limit or time.

These words are broken—never closing the gap
from which everything appears.

But for those whose hearts divine
whose whole bodies are prayers
I speak them here for you.

Navigation by Scent

These late days
my skin smells of roses
when nothing in me is constrained or
out of place.
So different from the
fenugreek, sea, sugar
skin of youth.

I've navigated life
by the scent of every house and room
smells of illness or an open heart
of disappointment
nervousness
and rage.

The banquet of morning and wet pine
layered scents in a crowded place
perfumes of life that spread
or clear or sit heavy on the mind
or like cannabis
that cling and coerce

I told my landlord:
The cedar in the yard smells like California.
The kitchen's reclaimed wood
smells clean and like
a magically bigger space.

These scents are memorialized:
people pretending to be someone else
drips of gasoline
East Bay golden hills in summer
eucalyptus trees baking in the sun
mugwort
saffron
agar
cardamom, freshly ground
helichrysum
jasmine
all the smells of God.

Also airports
baby hair
distant musk
deep inside the spines of books
art deco roadside motels
unwashed sheep's wool
the purest milk
and transmission fluid leaked
in the manifold
and burning.

Let Me Be the Incense

Let me be the incense
that burns up in offering.
Let there be nothing left but
silken fragrant ash.
Let the ash be spread
where food needs to grow.
And may everything that grows
nourish and serve anew.

A Crack in Time

Gaza Mo(u)rning

I wake up.
The neighborhood is full of sunlight and birds.
I make my tea and start scrolling the
buildings and bodies
bombed while I was sleeping.
Then some mornings I just have to bow down.
On the kitchen table
I rest my forehead in my hands
and begin to pray.

I Have a Catalog in My Heart

a poem that began writing at 3 a.m.

I have a catalog in my heart:
a pair of bloody pink roller skates
a man smeared in the street with half a head
shredded flesh and clothing hanging from a fence
see-through plastic bags with
parts of people mixed up
a sneaker with a foot
torn at the ankle
still in it

a toddler on a hospital bed stares at
the tendons of his
blown-off leg
a late-term fetus glistens from crown to toe
exploded from its mother's womb
umbilical cord sheared
in the rubble

a torso limbless in the shape of a seal

a boy weeps
chasing the corpse of his father
gurney receding
a two-year old girl screams
barefoot and alone
on a bombed street

the injured splayed on bare
hospital floors
torn and bloody cardboard
beneath their heads
the fathers with their lifeless
children swathed in rags and blood

single hands reach from under the rubble
and other hands grasp to free them
children bloody and shaking
children bloody and shaking

The images don't come unbidden
but the catalog is here
whenever I want to open it and
look again

My whole body every cell
has turned into a tenderness
of heart and yearning
and I'm not sorry that I see
I'm not sorry I remember
I want to know exactly who we are
and what it is that
has been done and
cries out to be done

Speechless Poem for Speechless Time

I bought the olive oil from Jenin
that you could not afford even
before October times.
You prepare your food
what little there is
with cheap vegetable oil
delivered in boxes from the fields
of the same countries
that kill you.
From across lands and seas
we gaze at each other
while we cook—
me at my oven
you at your fire.
I hurt from
so much seeing
and love.

Things Worshippers Must See and Hear

Blue-lipped children shaking with shock and fear.
A hand rescued, torn from the wrist. Tendons dangling.
Shot by strutting soldiers. A man in the street on his knees.
Neighbors run toward bombs to recover their dead.

A newborn swaddled in brown dust.
Head askew. Neck partially severed.
Shouts and cries in the chasms
between detonations.
Phosphorous-burned limbs.
Bodies made small by shredding.

They bleed on muddy hospital floors.
Sheets of copy paper cover their wounds.
Children seize. Tonic hands and feet curled.
Heads back. Eyes rolling.
Fresh blood glistens on the street.

Still alive, a face flashes from the ruins.
Neighbors dig with bare hands and reassuring words.
At every age, they call for God and their mothers.

The brave young journalist Bisan
cries for the loss of relics, libraries and
painless gatherings.

All of our tears are being written
in the blood and bones of the world.
Even those who turn away will not soon be forgetting.

Worship is the eyes meeting
what offers itself to be seen.
Worship is the ears meeting
what offers itself to be heard.
Worship is also the embrace
of what arrives and demands speaking.

Salt Water

People line up to pay for
salty water infested
with worms.
Children no older than three
drag heavy jugs down
ruined streets
exhausted feet shoeless and
tender in the rubble.
Friends on the livestreams
grow thinner.
They want us to see their
resilience and courage
but on days when
they break down
their tears are gifts to
our humanity.

I swear my heart is a bomb
on the brink of
detonation.
Not only for the
people of Gaza
but for the rest of us
and especially the ones
not seeing or
feeling these times.

Watch out!
My heart will explode
your cover
and turn it to rubble, too.

Jewels of God

for Mosab Abu Toha

Your tears are the jewels of God.
Your anger is God's sword.
Your patience is a miracle and
among the great proofs of the
value of a human incarnation.

Your grief is shredding the fabric of the world
to reveal the real world.
The fact that you keep on pleading
is an austerity beyond all austerities
and a mercy beyond all mercies.
God's mirror is ablaze in you.
The clarity with which it reflects
is hard to bear.

Since childhood, I have marched around
chanting and dancing to
songs of liberation.
I argued this or that point
and built sand castle solutions
out of enthusiasm, books, and air.

We were having fun
pumping ourselves up with
music and solidarity.

Now I'm heavy with
the sadness of these
late-stage revelations.
Now I seriously consider that
we may not survive
and that we are not winning
the easier way with our
delusions left
undestroyed.

Now I see that
if we want even
ordinary victory
we must call this
destruction and
descent by its real names
and bear thoroughly the
horror and
humanity of it all.

Mosab Abu Toha is a Gazan poet, teacher, and activist who managed to leave Gaza after being abducted by Israeli occupation forces in 2023. He now lives and teaches in the United States. He has published two books of poetry: *Things You May Find Hidden in My Ear* and *Forest of Noise*.

Humanity in Tents

If you speak or you don't speak.
If you learn or don't learn.
If you understand or condemn.
These atrocities
are marching into
our minds and blood and bones
into our schools and
friendships and homes
into our places of employment and
our shattered systems of law.

This time
if kinder more capacious hearts
do not prevail
one way or another
we will all be living in tents
and one kind of bomb or another
will fall.

When We Come to Rafah

I began this poem long ago
before the starving when
old olive groves and
bakeries were still
standing.

The title lingered without a poem
because these words already
were too full of yearning.
When we come to Rafah.
When we come to Rafah.

Back then, I imagined
your city would not be
so destroyed.

I imagined arriving
in time to share a coffee
and cook some meals.
I imagined many hands
gathered to
rebuild and
bury the dead.

Now I am wordless in grief
and each day it seems
less likely that
this poem will start
over again.

Rafah, once home to 250,000 Palestinians, is now devastated with the majority of its buildings bombed, crumbled, and blackened. The destruction has been described as absolute.

You Are Not Coming

Friends, we have waited here too long
and still you aren't coming
to speak for the ones we are harming
to speak for the ones we are killing
to speak for the young ones bleeding
and dying
to speak for the tender and righteous
and starving.

Friends, you are worried
for what you are losing
now and possibly in the future.
Because lands and cities and people are fragile,
you've always been scared
and hidden in grieving
and you choose to go inward or elsewhere
and you are not coming.

Call yourself radical, liberal, progressive, feminist
reasonable, spiritual, or just apprehensive.
Friends, your silence is truthful.
Your few words are hurtful.
Our hearts and our arms grow stronger
and you will need us
because you are weaker.

Friends, you are distant but
closer. I see you more clearly.
And I see you aren't coming.

I see you aren't coming
to defend the children and
fight with the warriors.
I see you aren't coming
to open the borders.
And when prison gates close
and bombs fall
when we are also
raped
silenced
and beaten
when we have to hide, but for different reasons
now I know you aren't coming.

And I know
a woman who loves women
born Jewish but
practicing freedom
beyond reasons and
empires and
doctrines of feeling.
And I've learned
I am also
Palestinian.
And you will not be coming.

Spring in Portland

I see red through the open weave of
my Japanese curtain.
First thought: the neighbor left
red Christmas lights in the vines
climbing the trellis by his door.
Second thought: Red flowers!
Portland's early spring delivers
shocking bursts of color overnight.
Third thought:
Blood from wounds in Gaza.
Red-stained streets, clothing, walls, and
bloodied sacks of flour
not flowers.

Petrichor Heartbreak

Heartbroken like Mount St. Helens
when the thistle grows again from
burnt soil.
Heartbroken like an infinity sky after
a category five storm.
Heartbroken like animal sounds
from the smoking remains
of careless forest fires.
Heartbroken like the sleep that comes
when you've seen everything
you desperately did not want to see.
Heartbroken like when the worst arrives
and there is nothing left to fear.
Heartbroken like the raw intimacy of grief shared.
Heartbroken like the heart harshly broken open.
Heartbroken like millions of hearts broken together.
Heartbroken like God's petrichor
after a drowning rain.

The Tortilla Survival Protocol

I didn't see it coming
but in the midst of all this
I kissed a fresh tortilla
and whispered close
into its fragrant skin
"Thank you for still being
sweet and simple."

I know that confusion and rage
helplessness
and desperation
don't go away until
their end times
naturally arrive.
But by filling
our mouths
with any name of God
we give these
a smaller place
and don't feel completely
inadequate and fucked.
Om namah shivaya

Likewise
offering small
services to others daily is
a medicine

that reaches deep into our
tissues with messages
of who we are
and who we will be
when the smoke
scatters and the sky is
easier to see.

If we keep kissing tortillas
roll mantras in our mouths
and offer ourselves
to each other as gifts
we can survive any confusions
smoke and fires
not necessarily intact
but who asked for *that* anyway?

What They Carry

Sometimes they carry water,
small children picking up and putting down
heavy plastic jugs over and over again in the heat.
Sometimes they carry lentils cooked outdoors
ladled into never-enough bowls.
Their pinched faces
worry that the food
will spill before reaching its
starved destination.
Sometimes they run
the injured draped in their arms
limp limbs dangling and blood
anointing the bombed stones.
Sometimes they carry the dead
wrapped in blood-stained shrouds
and cries of anger, sadness, and disbelief.
Sometimes they lift shredded body parts into
plastic bags
performing this service
with a certain quantity of
dignified reverence
and rage.
Sometimes they leap from the high rubble
onto the sand
carrying their bodies
in parkour arcs
of defiance and joy.

Sometimes they carry their tunes
across the ruined cities
across the oceans
reaching the lands of their assassins
and my ears.

Fresh Magic

Freshly killed babies
whole and anointed
with shining jewels of blood
still look so sweet
only a little unalived
as if they could re-
animate at any moment
and their open, generous smiles could return
if only I blinked
in just the right way.

But even by such
magical means
their deaths could
not be erased.
They could only
rewind like a film
where you've already
gotten to the end
and then you return
to an earlier time
because these
murdered children
cannot be unseen.

Aging Revolutionary

What can I do but
write poetry
send money
try to move a few people
and pray and weep?

I'm growing old and with a bum hip
I can't march around much or
dig the beloveds out
from under the rubble.
But I'll gladly come to Gaza
and help rebuild
if I won't be
more trouble than I'm worth.

Let me know!
When that wonderful time arrives
I can be there
even if you just want
another one to cook
or hug anyone who
asks.

Rations

for Hamada Shaqoura

Ten men share one can of beans.
It's all they will eat this day.
A young girl with starvation
belly and translucent arms.
Her face is etched and sad.
She turns away from the camera.
We won't meet her again.

A toddler runs alone through ruins, shrieking.
I have no words for this sound.
Horrible to even imagine
what she has seen.

Five days under siege with no food or water.
Emerging, the family is shot dead.
My tongue feels dry.

A father holds his dying child and weeps.
Her wrongly-angled limbs dangle down.

Hamada cooks
in his makeshift
kitchen with huge pots
rows of aluminum trays
and open fires.

He recreates his
Motherland's food
out of canned and powdered rations
and he speaks with the gift of his
angry eyes.

Only when Hamada feeds the children
does he permit the camera
to capture his sweet and
generous smile.

Hamada Shaqoura is a Gazan food blogger and activist turned community chef.

303 Days

This morning I read the headline
"Gazan flesh."
In the photo
two dusty hands hold
a brass tray
to the camera eye.

I imagine this tray
in former times
hoisting sandwiches at a
gathering of friends.

And I have already scrolled on before
my mind registers truly
the oblong lumps of blackened flesh
the stripes of red-burnt tendon
the Gazan flesh

before I see
the dusty hands
lift these remains
one-by-one tenderly
and place them on the tray
for offering.

336 Days

A plastic bag kite in the wind
I lost my glasses, he weeps
toddler's feet burning in the sand.
No soap, no shampoo, batteries dead
the smell of dead friends rotting in the street.
We dig for hours with our bare hands.
We sleep in the rubble of our homes.
Three-hundred thirty-six days
of the world seeing, knowing.

Motaz Wrote

Motaz wrote:
"Running out of options is not called resilience."
When living hangs so close to the edge of dying
when we're held down to the extremes
we humans are made of
let's build a holy place for that.
Let's open the temples in our hearts
to the burning cries, to the pain
completely raw and naked.
Let's not celebrate "resilience"
at the cost of other abandonings.

Motaz Azaiza is a Palestinian photojournalist from Gaza. He left Gaza early in 2024 and has continued to document the genocide and advocate for Palestinian self-determination and liberation. He is one of four Palestinian journalists to be nominated for a Nobel Peace Prize.

I Realize This is Not a Poem

I woke up this morning, and as I took my first sip of tea, I saw a man pick a severed hand out of the rubble.

The index finger pointed straight out, frozen in command. Run! Run! At the end of the wrist, tendons and flesh shredded, dangling.

Moments later, I saw a young girl, still alive, with flayed skin, or maybe it was burnt or boiled from the waist down including her vagina.

Then I saw a young boy with half an arm, amputated and bandaged.

The kind interviewer asked: "What do you want?"

The boy answered: "I want to be able to travel and get a new arm so I can play and help my mother."

"Where is your arm?" the interviewer asked.

"It's in heaven. It got to heaven before me."

This needed to be somewhere, so I wrote it here.

Don't Let Me Look

In Gaza this morning, I saw a dead baby.
Erased face and limbs. Charred black all over.

In the café this morning, I see a young father, radiant
with his two toddlers.

Cute clothes, I think, returning their easy smiles.

Mama is a barista. She leans in to kiss their father
across the counter. The kids jump up and down
excited to reach her.

Unbidden I see
the children of Gaza
amputated, shaking, bleeding, exploded.
I see them emerge from *your* babies like hauntings.

I see your kids screaming
exposed and lonely.
I see their skulls splintered.
I see them burned and broken.

We who see the murder
of Gazan children clearly
understand there is no refuge
for your children either.

If you want me to stop
writing poems like this one
keep your eyes closed
and don't let me look at your children.

Day 277 Exquisite Corpse

One morning on Instagram, I gathered the following words into a poem. These are the words of Palestinians experiencing genocide in Gaza.

A journey of displacement without a destination.
We are living a nightmare. Is this real?
Horrors and atrocities shake the heart and pull tears from our eyes.
We try to make something out of almost nothing.
We have returned to the stone age.
I'm swatting flies from my brother.
He is dying from lack of food before my eyes.
Can you not hear our screams?
The depravity seems never-ending.
Where is the good heart?
Ya Allah please end this sadness.
We need to be protected.
Stop this waterfall of blood.

Tenderness in the Rubble

Tenderness in the rubble.
Many hands lifting with care.
All around, fires igniting.
Even so, gentle, reassuring words.
My heart pulls in many directions.
My eyes see with a clarity that burns.
This is who we are.
Bombing the ones god sends as teachers
of the life and the way.

Another Sweet Boy is Dead

Another sweet boy is dead.
A bomb we made killed him.
The humans of Earth tried to save him.
But we held them back.
We aren't that place
we sing about in songs
or celebrate with hyperbole
and joy.
We are *this* place,
the place that kills
without remorse
a child and many more
since we came and stole
the homes and lands
of others.

Suzy and the Genociders

for Ahmed Aaed

I said how in the midst of this
live-streamed slaughter
I marvel at the bonds of friendship
growing between us.

Here we are.
Another canceled Christmas in Bethlehem.
And now, after fifteen months of friendship
and horror
we find ourselves sweetly bound
to Suzy, your tabby kitten
the beloved of the
caring people of Earth.

Suzy died on Christmas Eve
from one of those starvation
illnesses visited on the
people and animals
of Gaza.

Last time I checked Instagram,
one hundred twenty thousand humans
from every country
share your grief.
The genociders will not prevail.

Ahmed Aaed is a young boy from Gaza who loves cats and growing food for his family. On New Year's Day 2025, members of Ahmed's immediate family were injured by an Israeli bombing, and his small farm was destroyed along with its resident duck. Ahmed has vowed to plant again once things get better.

Those Who Cannot Tolerate Beauty

Our god is an enjoyer of
the beauty of all beings and things.
Our god's rapture is
a falling
for the glamorousness
of the creation.
Feeling abandoned
those who fall too far from god
learn to hate god's
magical ornamentation.

I know this from
the sad ones who have
tried to kill
the sweetness
the freedom in me.
They painfully exist
tortured by desires
to destroy what they want
and what they love.

I know this from the
sapphire sky
aqua sea
and dusty green of
newly-planted
olive trees

that frame more
fragile scenes of
Gaza's decimation.

I know this from
exquisite Gazan faces
old and young
mourning and dead
alive and dancing
and the rage of those who
over and over again
fail to extinguish
their light.

Drowning and Jasmine

I had to put dawn jasmine
on my crown.
I had to put night jasmine
on my brow and heart and wrists.
I had to remember the
sweet wealth
of life's cascade.

I see the richness here
but sometimes the poetry
the scent
eludes me.

Each day brings
fresh revelations of our genius
for inflicting
horrors on ourselves
and our world.

This grief drowns us all.

Still the jasmine flows
and the truth is
we are all eventually
swept away
in the river of that
infinite perfume.

Blast Zone

My heart is a blast zone.
This is the fruit of troubles.
We can only avoid troubles
by building walls and
creating new troubles.
If you try to rise above troubles
you'll be floating in air
with nothing underneath your feet.

Now I am crying at every ordinary thing.
A lonely face passing in the street
the friend of a friend's miscarriage
a kind moment, even on the screen
the longing to speak when no words come
and there is only a trembling.
These tears are falling
an abhisheka, a blessing, grace.
I wish the same for you.

We Run to Us

When the journalist Motaz
was still in Gaza
in the neighborhood where
he lived before the genocide
displaced him
the Israelis bombed his
neighbor's building.

Motaz was running.
The street, a blur of rubble
careened with the camera
bouncing on his chest.
Screams and shouts all around him.
Smoke and dust rising.

I could hear Motaz's ragged
breath full of adrenaline and fear.
I was sure he ran from the
explosions to stay alive.
But then I realized he was
running toward them.
He was running toward them.
And other men were running
toward the explosions too, and
toward the bombed building,
still smoking.

The next thing I saw:
hands reaching to dig
reaching out to dig in the
smoking rubble.
And another hand reaching up
from underneath.
A single hand reaching.

If we want to survive and grow
into any life worth living
we have to run toward each other.
We have to run to each other
in the midst of whatever
bombing
toward the hands that are reaching from
whatever rubble
they find themselves
buried under.

Acknowledgments

Many thanks to Mere Elzea and Tess Brown Lavoie for their assistance with design and editing, respectively. And much gratitude to the readers of kindred108.love whose subscriptions paid for the design and layout of this book.

Infinite thanks to the teachers who have graced my life and, through their example, have taught me that the fruit of practice is to be oneself in the fullest sense.

About Shambhavi

Shambhavi Sarasvati is the spiritual director of Jaya Kula, a nonprofit community offering opportunities to learn and practice in the direct realization traditions of Trika Shaivism and Dzogchen. Jaya Kula is located in Portland, Oregon. Find out more about Jaya Kula and Shambhavi's teaching schedule at jayakula.org.

Shambhavi holds an M.F.A. in Creative Writing from Mills College and a Ph.D. in Modern Thought and Literature from Stanford University. Before founding Jaya Kula, Shambhavi taught comparative literature and new media studies at Northwestern University. She is the author of an academic book about posthumanism and seven books about spiritual life and practice. These days, much of her creative output can be found at kindred108.love.

www.ingramcontent.com/pod-product-compliance
Lightning Source LLC
Chambersburg PA
CBHW030556080526
44585CB00012B/394